Published by Smart Apple Media,
an imprint of Black Rabbit Books
P.O. Box 3263, Mankato, Minnesota 56002
www.blackrabbitbooks.com

Published by arrangement with
The Salariya Book Company Ltd

Cataloging-in-Publication Data is available
from the Library of Congress

Printed in the United States
At Corporate Graphics,
North Mankato, Minnesota

9 8 7 6 5 4 3 2 1

ISBN: 978-1-62588-337-7

Illustrators: Carolyn Scrace
Nicholas Hewetson
Pamela Hewetson
David Antram

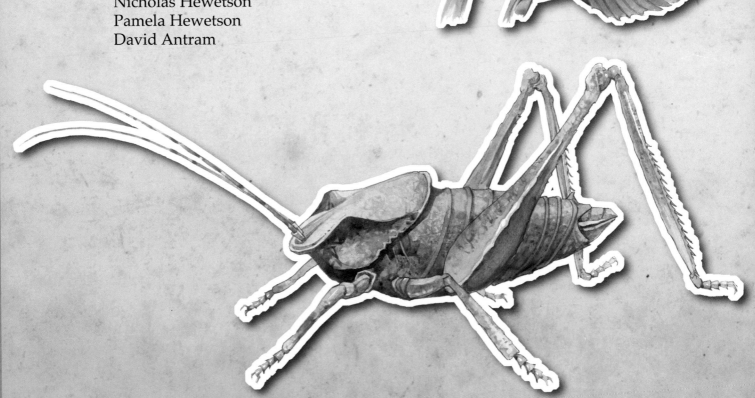

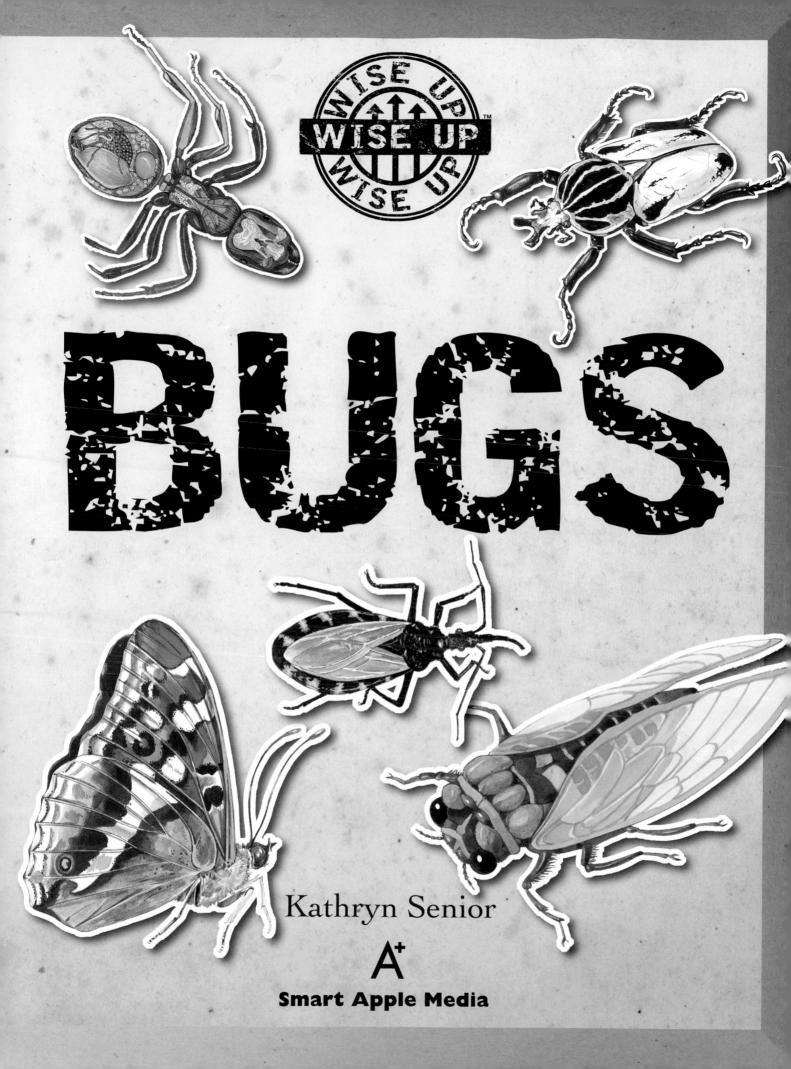

BUGS

Kathryn Senior

A+

Smart Apple Media

Contents

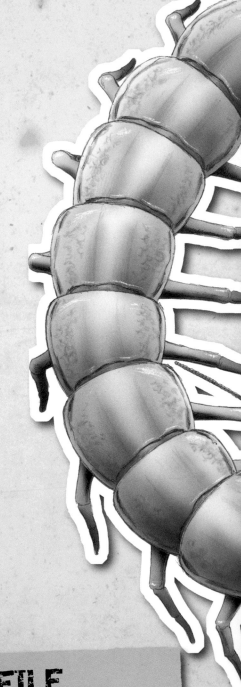

FACTFILE
ARTHROPODS
• The phylum Arthropoda (*arthro* = joint, *poda* = foot) is the largest phylum in the animal kingdom. It includes about 75% of all species.
• Centipedes eat soft-bodied insects, earthworms and slugs.

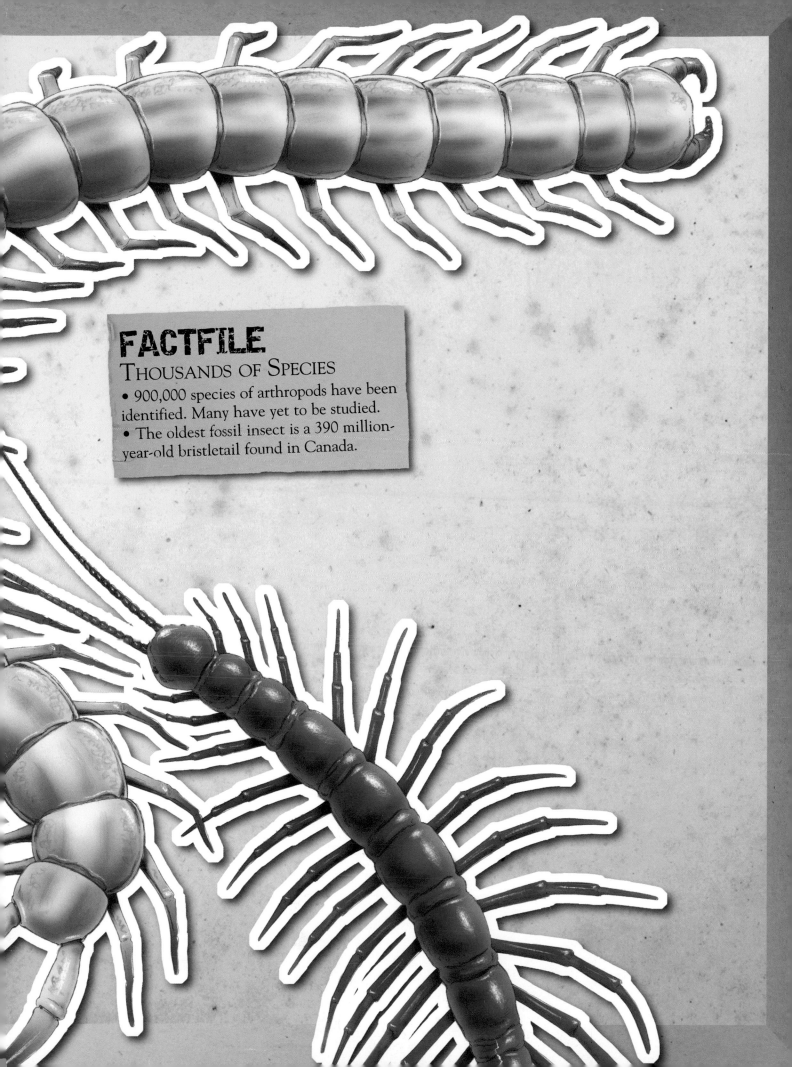

FACTFILE
THOUSANDS OF SPECIES

• 900,000 species of arthropods have been identified. Many have yet to be studied.

• The oldest fossil insect is a 390 million-year-old bristletail found in Canada.

What Are Bugs?

▼ Arthropods are a group of animals with segmented bodies and tough outer skeletons. They are subdivided according to their features.

Phylum: Arthropoda

Subphylum: Chelicerata

Class: Arachnida (spiders, ticks, and mites)

Class: Merostomata (horseshoe crabs)

Class: Pycnogonida (sea spiders)

Subphylum: Crustacea

Subphylum: Uniramia

Class: Chilopoda (centipedes)

Class: Diplopoda (millipedes)

Class: Insecta (flies, wasps, bees, beetles, butterflies, moths)

This book concentrates on Arachnida (spiders, ticks, and mites), centipedes, millipedes, and insects. Insects include flies, wasps, bees, beetles, moths, dragonflies, and butterflies. Let's start by having a closer look at some of the main characteristics of arachnids and insects.

Which are the biggest, fastest, longest, smallest, noisiest, most dangerous, and most revolting bugs and minibeasts? The bugs in this book are not all insects but they are all arthropods. It's a good idea to know what the difference is. The diagram on the left shows how the group of animals called arthropods is divided up.

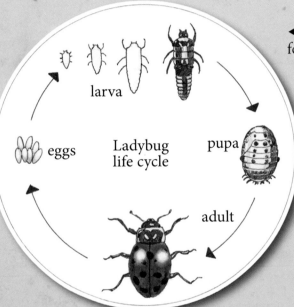

larva

eggs

Ladybug life cycle

pupa

adult

◀ Some insects, ladybugs for example, experience what is called complete metamorphosis. They start life as an egg, which hatches into a larva. The larva sheds its skin several times as it grows. It then changes into a pupa. A few days later an adult ladybug emerges.

▶ Other insects, such as this flower bug, just grow bigger. This life cycle is called incomplete metamorphosis, because the change is gradual. The egg develops into a larva, called a nymph. The nymph sheds its skin repeatedly as it grows into an adult.

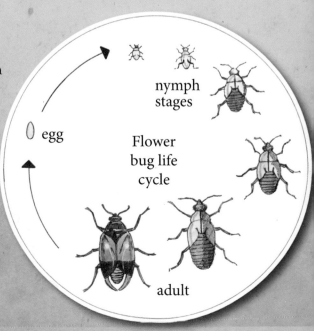

egg

nymph stages

Flower bug life cycle

adult

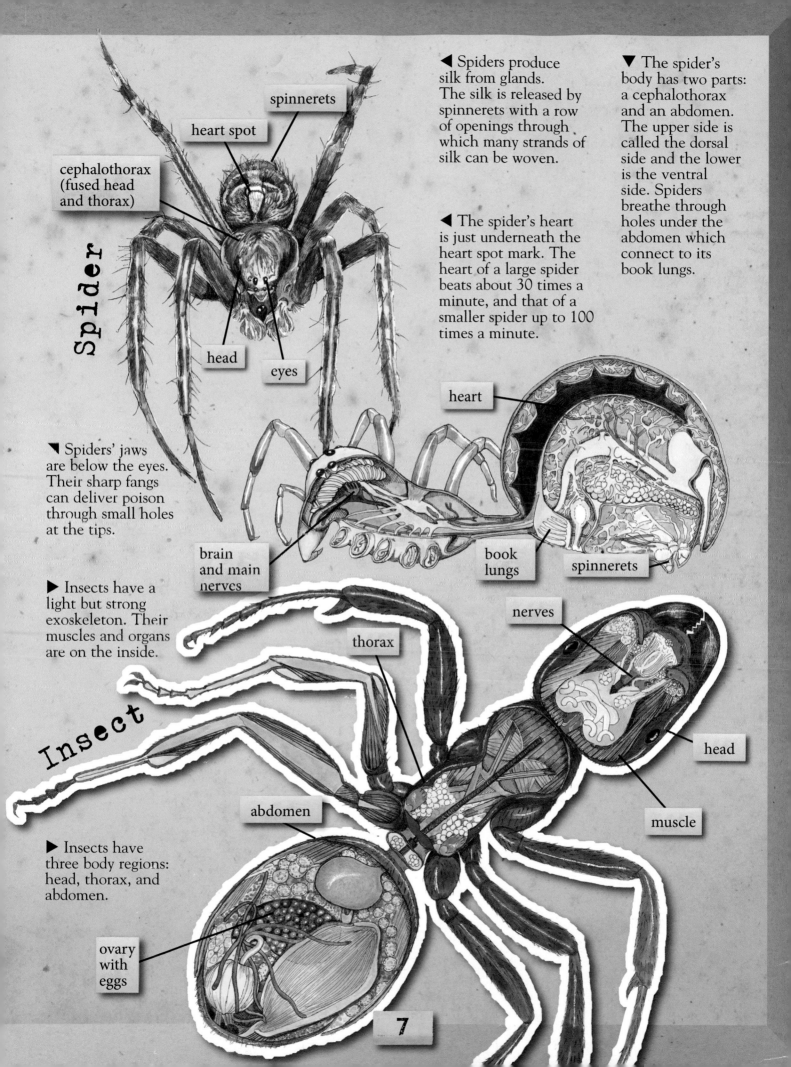

Spider

spinnerets

heart spot

cephalothorax (fused head and thorax)

head

eyes

◄ Spiders produce silk from glands. The silk is released by spinnerets with a row of openings through which many strands of silk can be woven.

▼ The spider's body has two parts: a cephalothorax and an abdomen. The upper side is called the dorsal side and the lower is the ventral side. Spiders breathe through holes under the abdomen which connect to its book lungs.

◄ The spider's heart is just underneath the heart spot mark. The heart of a large spider beats about 30 times a minute, and that of a smaller spider up to 100 times a minute.

◄ Spiders' jaws are below the eyes. Their sharp fangs can deliver poison through small holes at the tips.

heart

brain and main nerves

book lungs

spinnerets

▶ Insects have a light but strong exoskeleton. Their muscles and organs are on the inside.

nerves

thorax

head

muscle

abdomen

▶ Insects have three body regions: head, thorax, and abdomen.

Insect

ovary with eggs

7

Scary Spiders

There are over 60,000 different species of spiders around the world. Spiders are carnivores: they eat insects and other small animals. Most spiders kill their prey by injecting them with poison. They then spray the dead body with digestive juices and suck up the resulting liquid. A row of fine hairs just inside the spider's mouth filters out any lumps. Other spiders don't use poison, but simply spray the trapped insect with digestive juices —they digest the prey to death. The black widow, the tarantula, the brown recluse, the funnel-web, and the redback are dangerous to humans.

Tarantula

spinnerets

abdomen

body hairs

▼ The poisonous redback is from Australia. Only the female is large enough to bite a human. A victim can become seriously ill.

Redback

◀ The black widow spider is common in Europe and North America. Its venom is 15 times more poisonous than rattlesnake venom and kills one in every hundred victims.

Black widow

▶ A brown recluse spider's stinging bite is very painful. The venom kills the skin and muscle around the bite, leaving a hole that takes weeks to heal.

Brown recluse

Funnel-web

▲ The funnel-web is one of the most dangerous spiders in Australia. The male is more dangerous because he wanders above ground while the female rarely leaves her funnel-shaped burrow.

► Tarantulas are the largest of all spiders. They eat large insects and even small birds and mammals. Their venom is not fatal to humans but they can give a nasty bite. They can flick their short body hairs and if these get into the eyes, they can blind.

cephalothorax

eyes

fangs

Orb spider

▲ Orb spiders make wheel webs with spokes like a wheel and a sticky thread that spirals around. Making such a complex web uses up a lot of silk and energy. One species of orb spider can build a web in under an hour using about 65 feet (20 m) of silk.

Webs

Spiders use silk to trap their prey by making trip wires or elaborate webs that catch flying insects with their sticky, almost invisible threads. The silk comes from glands in the spider's abdomen. The liquid silk hardens in air into a gluey thread. It is made of protein, so when a web is damaged the spider eats the silk before making a new one. Spiders also use their silk to wrap up prey to eat later and to make egg sacs to keep their young safe until they hatch.

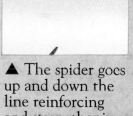

▲ To start the web, an orb spider releases a thread. When it sticks to something, the first bridge of the web is formed.

▲ The spider goes up and down the line reinforcing and strengthening it with extra lines. She then produces a second thread.

▲ She attaches this new thread to another point. This Y-shape forms the first three spokes of the web.

▲ Four outer threads are spun to form the frame of the web. These might be attached to nearby twigs.

▲ The rest of the spokes are spun and a sticky thread is then woven between them.

▲ The web usually lasts just one night. The spider then eats it but leaves the first thread in place.

Dynastes beetle

▲ This is one of the largest beetles in the world. The males are 7.5 inches (19 cm) long.

Mega Beetles

Beetles come in every shape, color, and size. Like all insects, they have a head, a thorax with six legs, and an abdomen. Their bodies are covered by a suit of armor called an exoskeleton which protects them from predators. Many types of beetle clear up the waste left by other animals and plants. They lay their eggs in the dead bodies of animals so their hatching larvae can feed on the decaying material. However, some beetles are serious pests. The elm bark beetle carries a fungus that causes Dutch elm disease, a deadly disease that in many countries has wiped out nearly all of the elm trees. Deathwatch beetles damage houses and the Colorado potato beetle wrecks potato crops.

FACTFILE
BEETLES
• There are more than 360,000 named species of beetle.
• About 25 percent of all animal species are beetles.

Cockroach

▼ Dung beetles, like the Spanish crescent-horned dung beetle, clear up the feces of other animals.

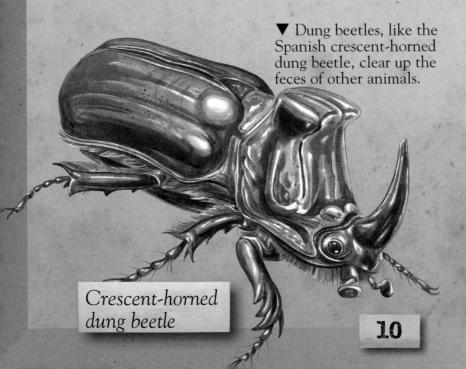

Crescent-horned dung beetle

◄ Mating pairs dig an underground den and then go off to look for a pile of fresh dung. They roll chunks of dung back to the den with their back legs. The female lays her eggs in several dung balls and the hatching larvae feed on it.

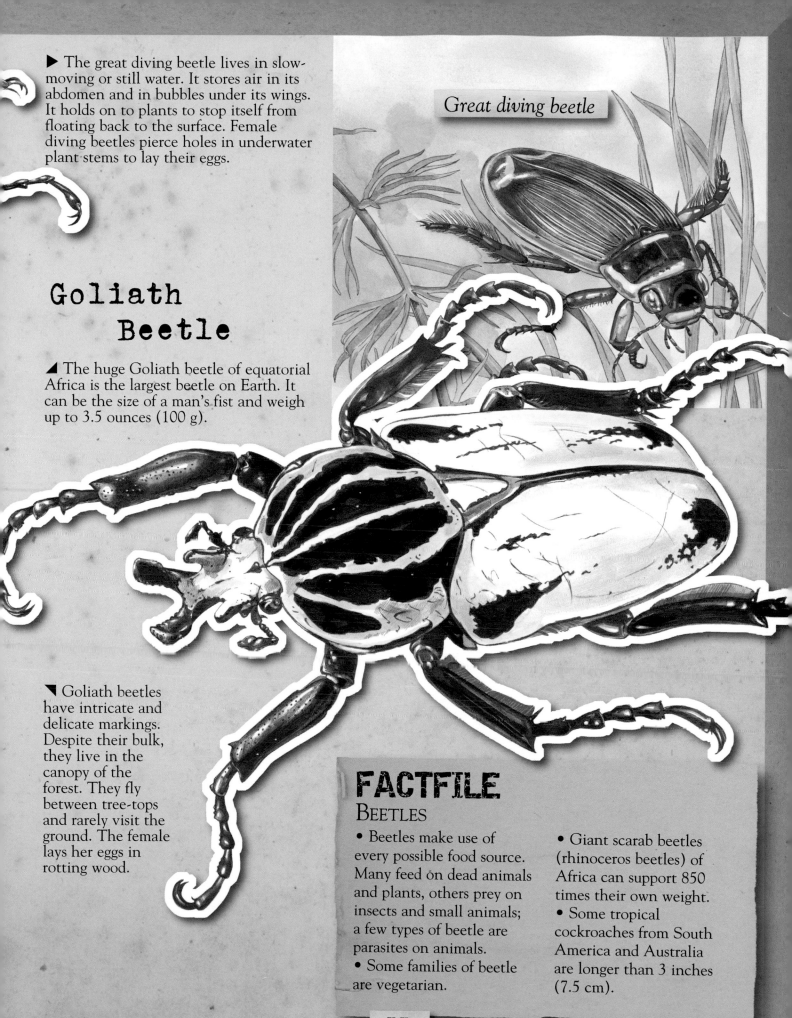

▶ The great diving beetle lives in slow-moving or still water. It stores air in its abdomen and in bubbles under its wings. It holds on to plants to stop itself from floating back to the surface. Female diving beetles pierce holes in underwater plant stems to lay their eggs.

Great diving beetle

Goliath Beetle

◢ The huge Goliath beetle of equatorial Africa is the largest beetle on Earth. It can be the size of a man's fist and weigh up to 3.5 ounces (100 g).

◣ Goliath beetles have intricate and delicate markings. Despite their bulk, they live in the canopy of the forest. They fly between tree-tops and rarely visit the ground. The female lays her eggs in rotting wood.

FACTFILE
BEETLES

• Beetles make use of every possible food source. Many feed on dead animals and plants, others prey on insects and small animals; a few types of beetle are parasites on animals.
• Some families of beetle are vegetarian.

• Giant scarab beetles (rhinoceros beetles) of Africa can support 850 times their own weight.
• Some tropical cockroaches from South America and Australia are longer than 3 inches (7.5 cm).

11

Beautiful Butterflies

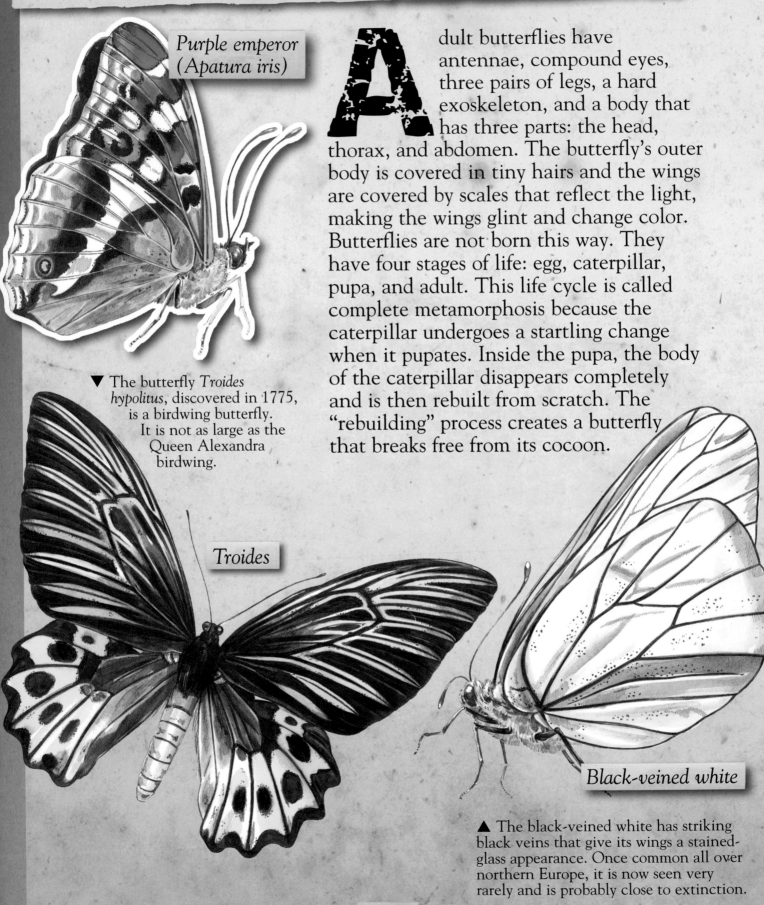

Purple emperor
(Apatura iris)

Adult butterflies have antennae, compound eyes, three pairs of legs, a hard exoskeleton, and a body that has three parts: the head, thorax, and abdomen. The butterfly's outer body is covered in tiny hairs and the wings are covered by scales that reflect the light, making the wings glint and change color. Butterflies are not born this way. They have four stages of life: egg, caterpillar, pupa, and adult. This life cycle is called complete metamorphosis because the caterpillar undergoes a startling change when it pupates. Inside the pupa, the body of the caterpillar disappears completely and is then rebuilt from scratch. The "rebuilding" process creates a butterfly that breaks free from its cocoon.

▼ The butterfly *Troides hypolitus*, discovered in 1775, is a birdwing butterfly. It is not as large as the Queen Alexandra birdwing.

Troides

Black-veined white

▲ The black-veined white has striking black veins that give its wings a stained-glass appearance. Once common all over northern Europe, it is now seen very rarely and is probably close to extinction.

FACTFILE
BUTTERFLIES

The wingspan of a female Queen Alexandra birdwing can reach almost 12 inches (30 cm).

◢ There are over 600 species of swallowtail butterflies in the world. They are brightly colored to put other insects off eating them, and to attract mates.

Swallowtail

Butterfly or moth? Butterflies are active by day, have clubbed antennae, and are brightly colored. Moths are nocturnal, their antennae are straight, and they tend to be drab in color.

▶ The Queen Alexandra birdwing is the largest butterfly in the world. It takes about four months to complete its life cycle from egg to adult butterfly. It then lives for just three months. Birdwings live in the rainforests of Papua New Guinea but are now very rare.

FACTFILE
BUTTERFLIES

• Butterflies and moths see ultraviolet light better than humans, so they see patterns on flower petals that we cannot.
• There are approximately 136,800 species of butterflies and moths in the world.

▶ A male Queen Alexandra birdwing has a yellow body with bluish-green markings on a black background. The female has brown wings with lighter spots.

Queen Alexandra birdwing

Light and Sound

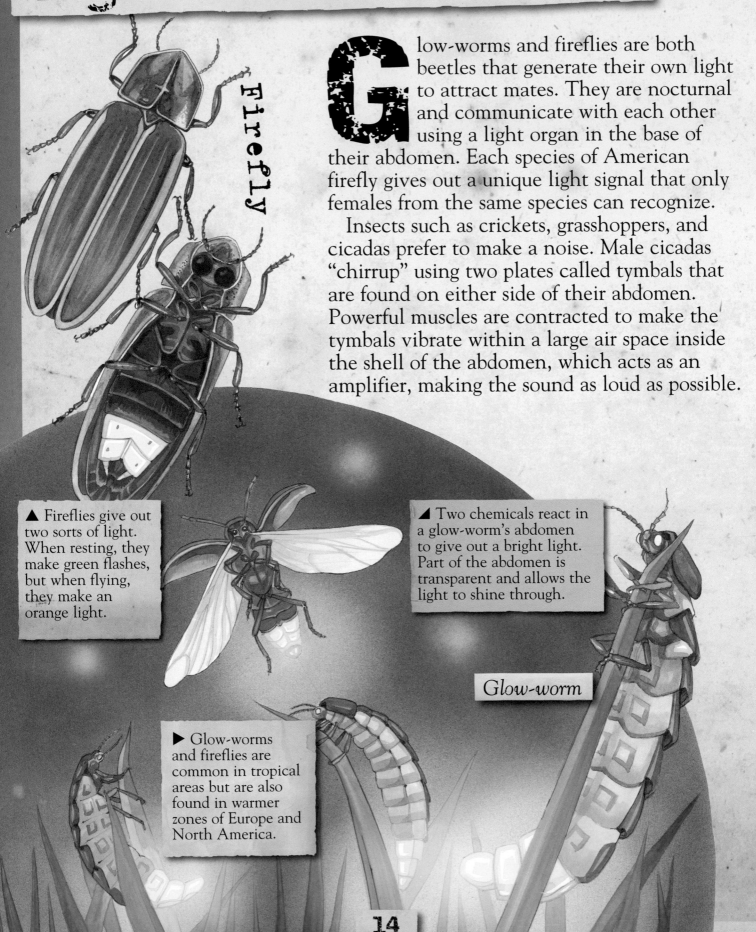

Glow-worms and fireflies are both beetles that generate their own light to attract mates. They are nocturnal and communicate with each other using a light organ in the base of their abdomen. Each species of American firefly gives out a unique light signal that only females from the same species can recognize.

Insects such as crickets, grasshoppers, and cicadas prefer to make a noise. Male cicadas "chirrup" using two plates called tymbals that are found on either side of their abdomen. Powerful muscles are contracted to make the tymbals vibrate within a large air space inside the shell of the abdomen, which acts as an amplifier, making the sound as loud as possible.

Firefly

▲ Fireflies give out two sorts of light. When resting, they make green flashes, but when flying, they make an orange light.

◀ Two chemicals react in a glow-worm's abdomen to give out a bright light. Part of the abdomen is transparent and allows the light to shine through.

Glow-worm

▶ Glow-worms and fireflies are common in tropical areas but are also found in warmer zones of Europe and North America.

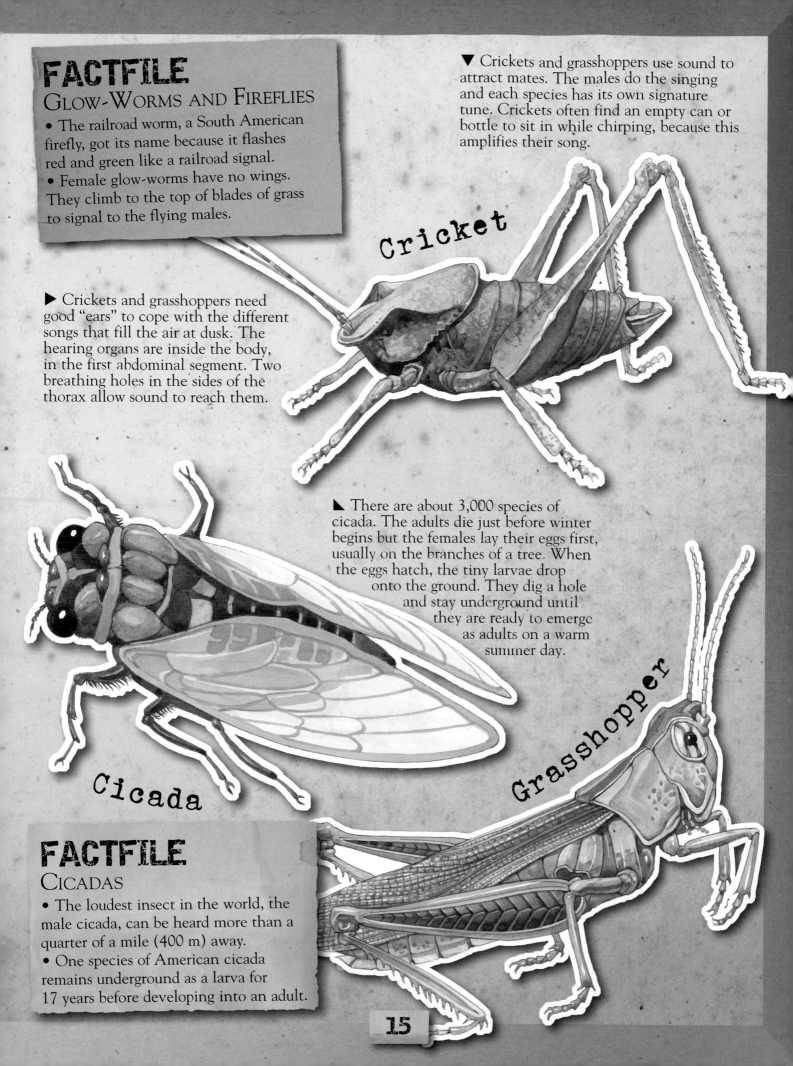

▼ Crickets and grasshoppers use sound to attract mates. The males do the singing and each species has its own signature tune. Crickets often find an empty can or bottle to sit in while chirping, because this amplifies their song.

Cricket

► Crickets and grasshoppers need good "ears" to cope with the different songs that fill the air at dusk. The hearing organs are inside the body, in the first abdominal segment. Two breathing holes in the sides of the thorax allow sound to reach them.

◢ There are about 3,000 species of cicada. The adults die just before winter begins but the females lay their eggs first, usually on the branches of a tree. When the eggs hatch, the tiny larvae drop onto the ground. They dig a hole and stay underground until they are ready to emerge as adults on a warm summer day.

Cicada

Grasshopper

Lots of Legs

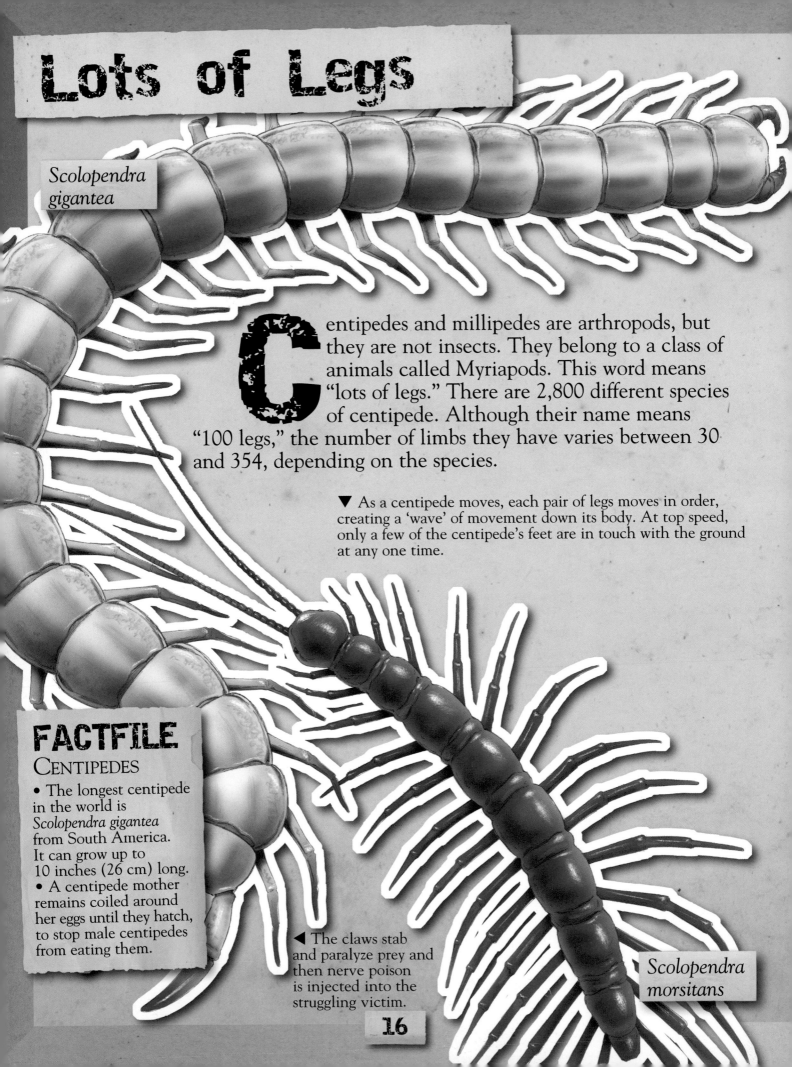

Scolopendra gigantea

Centipedes and millipedes are arthropods, but they are not insects. They belong to a class of animals called Myriapods. This word means "lots of legs." There are 2,800 different species of centipede. Although their name means "100 legs," the number of limbs they have varies between 30 and 354, depending on the species.

▼ As a centipede moves, each pair of legs moves in order, creating a 'wave' of movement down its body. At top speed, only a few of the centipede's feet are in touch with the ground at any one time.

FACTFILE
CENTIPEDES

• The longest centipede in the world is *Scolopendra gigantea* from South America. It can grow up to 10 inches (26 cm) long.
• A centipede mother remains coiled around her eggs until they hatch, to stop male centipedes from eating them.

◄ The claws stab and paralyze prey and then nerve poison is injected into the struggling victim.

Scolopendra morsitans

▶ The body of a millipede is covered with hard plates of cuticle that overlap, forming tough body armor. The plates are jointed so the millipede can curl itself into a tight ball.

Millipede

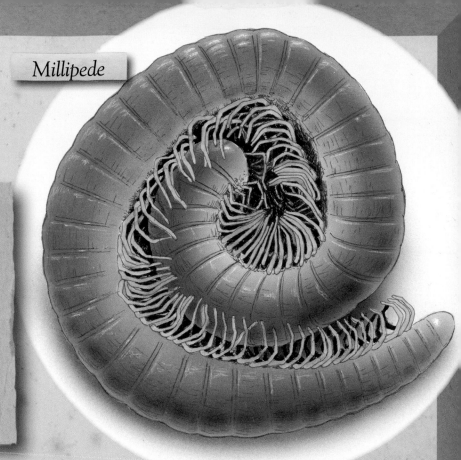

FACTFILE
MILLIPEDES

• The largest millipede in the world is *Archispirostreptus gigas* of Africa, which can be up to 12 inches (30 cm) long. It has a body diameter of 0.75 inch (2 cm).

• Millipedes usually eat decaying vegetation. Some eat the remains of dead animals, and a few tropical species suck juices from fruit.

• Millipedes live for between 1 and 6 years.

Millipedes are much gentler creatures than centipedes. They are slower-moving and are herbivores—they never hunt. There are about 7,500 known species of millipede. None have as many as a thousand legs, as their name suggests. In fact, millipedes never have more than 750 limbs. Millipedes like hot climates and some species are very sensitive to changes in temperature and moisture.

Centipede   *Millipede*

Millipede

▲ The number of segments in a millipede's body depends on the species, but most have between 10 and 100. Each segment has two pairs of legs, except the seventh segment which is modified for reproduction purposes.

▲ Centipedes have single body segments, with one pair of legs per segment. Millipedes have double segments, with two pairs of legs on each. So, a millipede has more legs for a given length.

Destructive Bugs

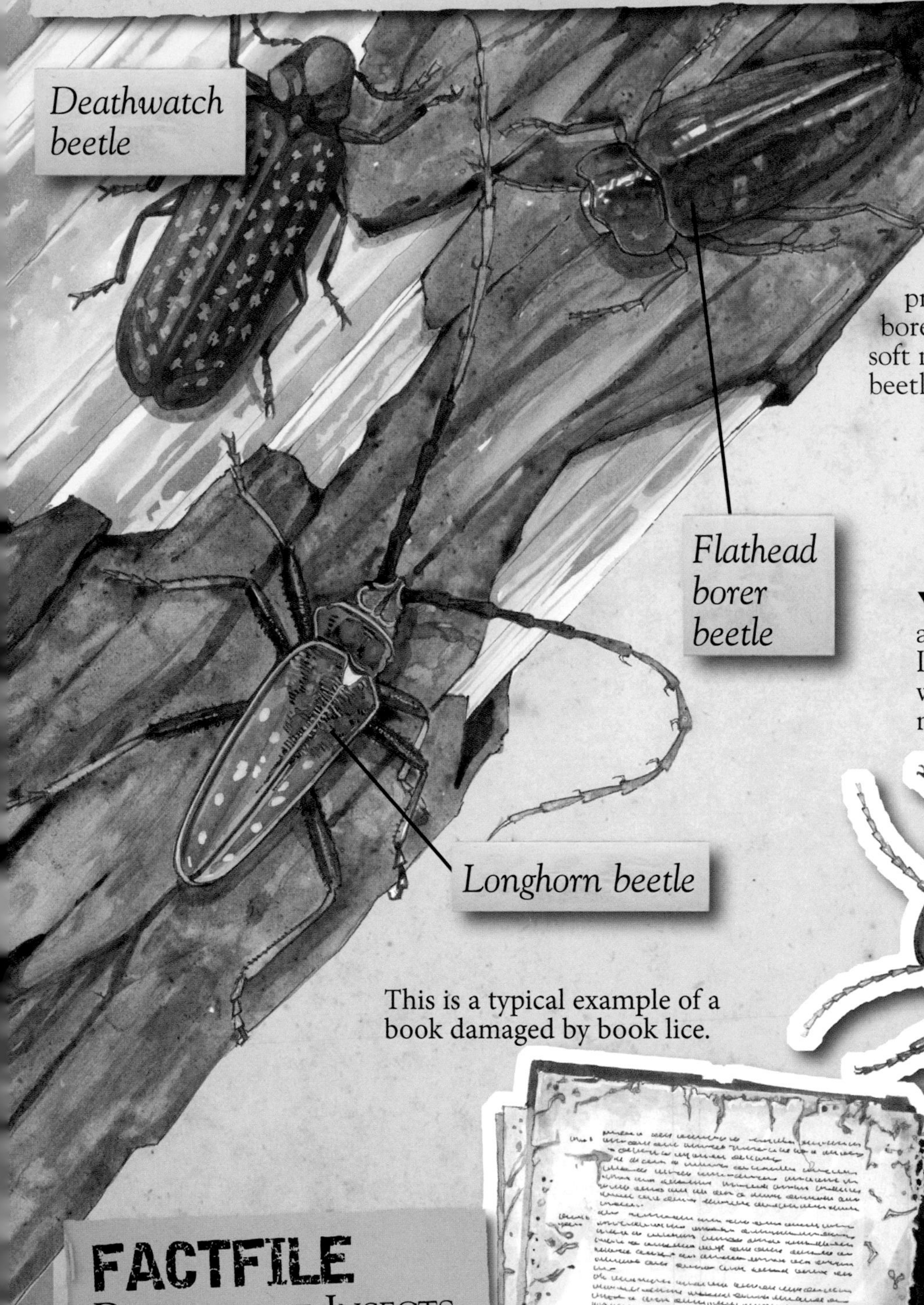

Deathwatch beetle

Flathead borer beetle

Longhorn beetle

◀ The most common wood-boring insects include the common furniture beetle, the deathwatch beetle, the wood-boring weevil, and the house longhorn. Wood-boring beetle larvae feed on wood and wood products. Adults of some species also bore holes into plaster, plastic, and even soft metals. Many species of wood-boring beetles feed only on living trees.

▼ The book louse lives in trees and shrubs or under bark or stones. It is a small, soft-bodied insect with mouthparts that are ideal for munching through old paper.

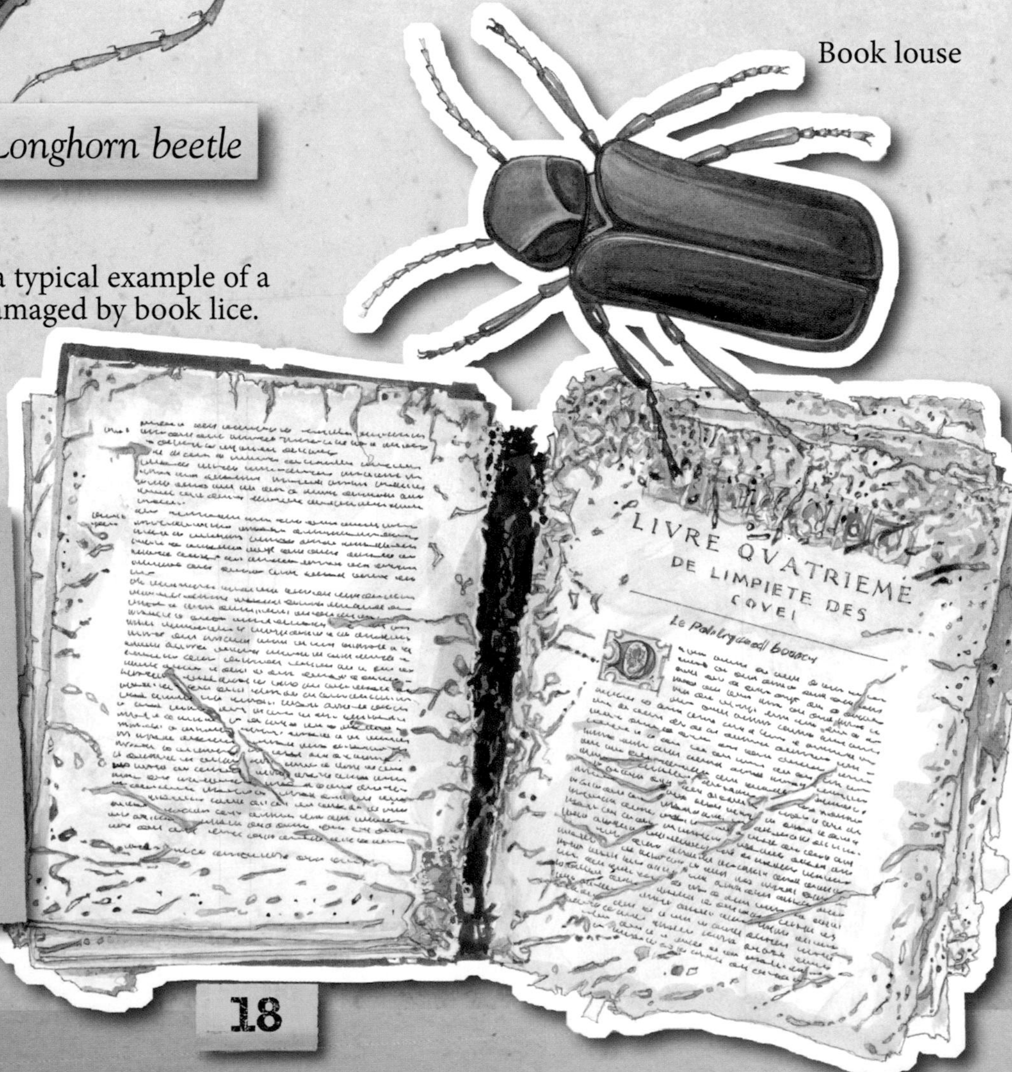

Book louse

This is a typical example of a book damaged by book lice.

FACTFILE
DESTRUCTIVE INSECTS
• More trees are lost to insects each year than are destroyed by forest fires.
• The short-circuit beetle can chew through electrical cables. This lets water in, causing short circuits.

▼ Adult Colorado potato beetles spend the winter in the soil or under leaf litter. They become active in May and lay eggs on the undersides of potato-plant leaves. The hatched larvae and adults feed on the foliage of the plants, causing extensive damage.

Colorado potato beetle

FACTFILE
LOCUSTS
• The most destructive insect in the world is the desert locust (*Schistocerca gregaria*).
• There can be as many as 40 billion desert locusts in a single swarm.
• The food eaten by a large swarm of desert locusts in one day could feed 400,000 people for one year.

Africa

▶ In the 20th century, one locust swarm traveled over most of the African continent. The dark red area shows where the swarm started and the arrows plot its spread over the next 12 years.

Some bugs are particularly damaging to humans. Desert locusts in swarms of over 620 miles (1,000 km) in width were recorded last century. The damage they do to crops and natural vegetation is incredible. Every plant for miles is stripped bare as they eat all available food. In African countries, where food may already be scarce because of drought or war, a plague of locusts can mean widespread starvation. Fortunately, many locusts die due to bad weather or are eaten by other animals.

Desert locusts

▶ Female locusts lay about 200 eggs during their lifetime. Once the young (hoppers) hatch, they eat low-lying plants. It is the fledgling locusts that swarm to find new sources of food and breeding grounds.

Bug Engineers

Honeybee hive

Honeybee hive

Termite mound

▲ A large hive has many closely packed combs. The bees make sure that no cell is unfilled.

▲ Honeybees usually build their hive in holes in tree trunks or gaps in rocks. The hive consists of many vertical walls of wax called combs. Every comb is made up of hundreds of six-sided cells, each tilted slightly, so that its contents do not fall out. The cells at the center of the hive house the eggs and larvae. The cells near the edges are used for storing honey. Pollen is stored in a ring of cells in between.

FACTFILE
TERMITES
• The largest termite in the world is nearly 5 inches (12 cm) in length.
• Some African termites have been known to live for up to 50 years.

Honeybees inside hive

FACTFILE
HONEYBEES
• Honeybees air-condition their hive when it gets too hot. Worker bees stand at the entrance and fan their wings to cool the air as it enters the hive.
• In its lifetime a worker honeybee collects enough nectar to make about 3 ounces (60 g) of honey.

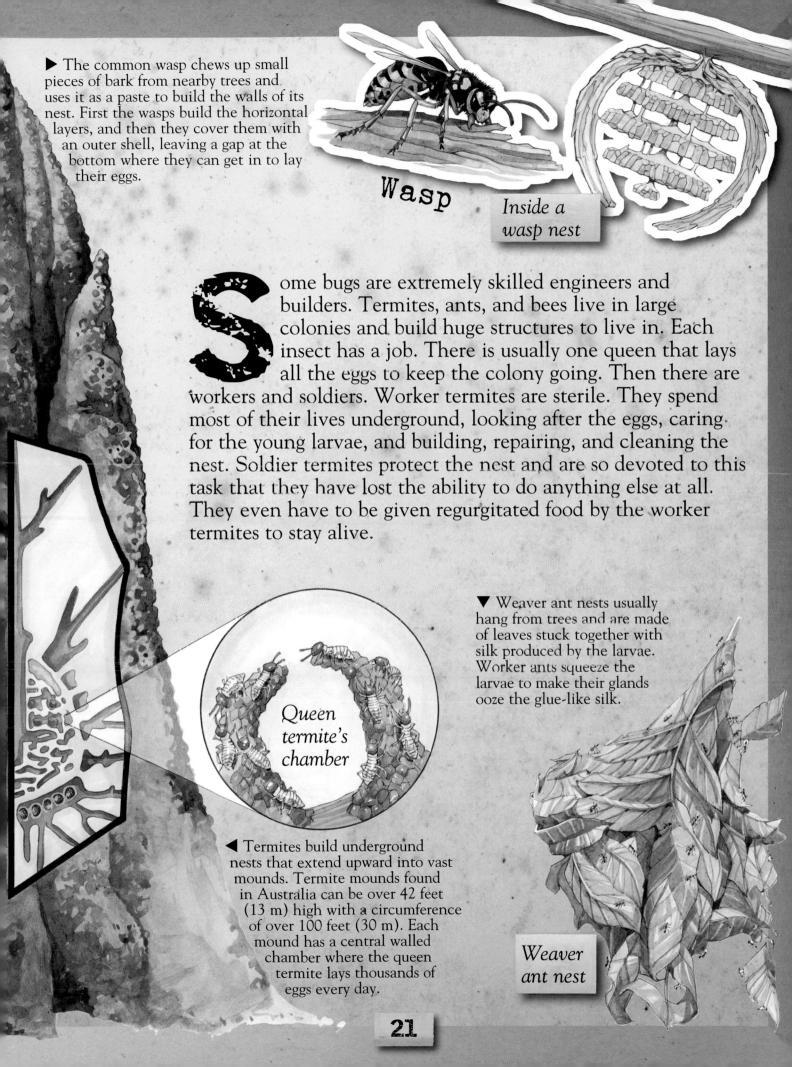

▶ The common wasp chews up small pieces of bark from nearby trees and uses it as a paste to build the walls of its nest. First the wasps build the horizontal layers, and then they cover them with an outer shell, leaving a gap at the bottom where they can get in to lay their eggs.

Wasp

Inside a wasp nest

Some bugs are extremely skilled engineers and builders. Termites, ants, and bees live in large colonies and build huge structures to live in. Each insect has a job. There is usually one queen that lays all the eggs to keep the colony going. Then there are workers and soldiers. Worker termites are sterile. They spend most of their lives underground, looking after the eggs, caring for the young larvae, and building, repairing, and cleaning the nest. Soldier termites protect the nest and are so devoted to this task that they have lost the ability to do anything else at all. They even have to be given regurgitated food by the worker termites to stay alive.

Queen termite's chamber

▼ Weaver ant nests usually hang from trees and are made of leaves stuck together with silk produced by the larvae. Worker ants squeeze the larvae to make their glands ooze the glue-like silk.

◀ Termites build underground nests that extend upward into vast mounds. Termite mounds found in Australia can be over 42 feet (13 m) high with a circumference of over 100 feet (30 m). Each mound has a central walled chamber where the queen termite lays thousands of eggs every day.

Weaver ant nest

21

It's Hard Being a Bug

Many bugs work hard just to survive. Ants, like termites, build large nests that have extremely complicated architecture. The senior ants release chemicals that control the worker ants, making them slave away without rest for most of their lives. Silk moths produce all the silk that we use and are the only domesticated insect. They have to work incredibly hard, controlled as they are by people.

Leaf-cutter ant

FACTFILE
HARD WORKERS
• Female mole crickets lay 200–300 eggs that take 20–30 days to hatch.
• Ant colonies can have as many as one million members.
• There are 14,000 different species of ant.

▼ Mole crickets have a tough carapace (hood) to protect them as they squeeze through tunnels.

abdomen

Mole cricket

◤ The mole cricket is a large burrowing insect that has front legs like those of a mole. Its powerful pad-like front feet with large spines shovel the earth to each side as it burrows.

carapace

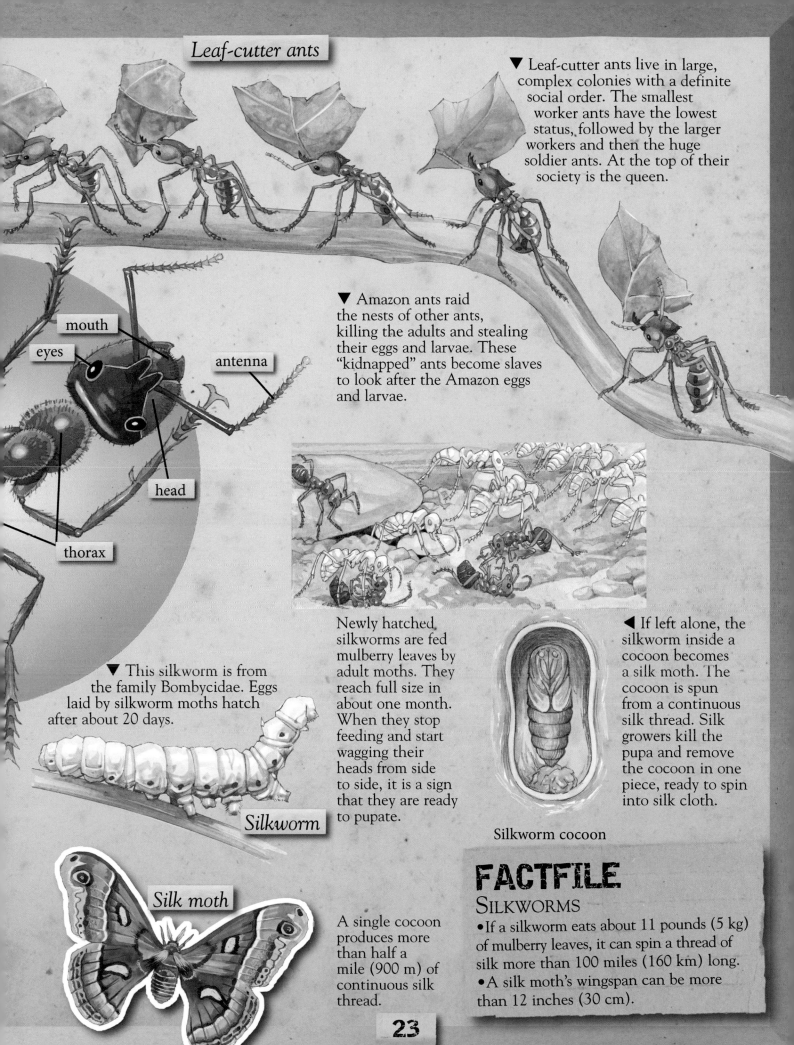

Leaf-cutter ants

▼ Leaf-cutter ants live in large, complex colonies with a definite social order. The smallest worker ants have the lowest status, followed by the larger workers and then the huge soldier ants. At the top of their society is the queen.

mouth

eyes

antenna

head

thorax

▼ Amazon ants raid the nests of other ants, killing the adults and stealing their eggs and larvae. These "kidnapped" ants become slaves to look after the Amazon eggs and larvae.

▼ This silkworm is from the family Bombycidae. Eggs laid by silkworm moths hatch after about 20 days.

Silkworm

Newly hatched silkworms are fed mulberry leaves by adult moths. They reach full size in about one month. When they stop feeding and start wagging their heads from side to side, it is a sign that they are ready to pupate.

◀ If left alone, the silkworm inside a cocoon becomes a silk moth. The cocoon is spun from a continuous silk thread. Silk growers kill the pupa and remove the cocoon in one piece, ready to spin into silk cloth.

Silkworm cocoon

Silk moth

A single cocoon produces more than half a mile (900 m) of continuous silk thread.

FACTFILE
SILKWORMS
• If a silkworm eats about 11 pounds (5 kg) of mulberry leaves, it can spin a thread of silk more than 100 miles (160 km) long.
• A silk moth's wingspan can be more than 12 inches (30 cm).

Magnificent Mothers

Many bugs make good parents. Aphids breed as if intending to take over the world! The female aphids hatch in early summer. These tiny insects are born pregnant and reproduce very quickly to take advantage of plentiful summer food. When the food supply decreases in late summer, the male aphids are born. These live just long enough to fertilize the eggs to guarantee next year's population of aphids.

The queen of a termite, ant, or bee colony also produces huge numbers of offspring. After mating, her body expands into a swollen bag of eggs that will repopulate the colony.

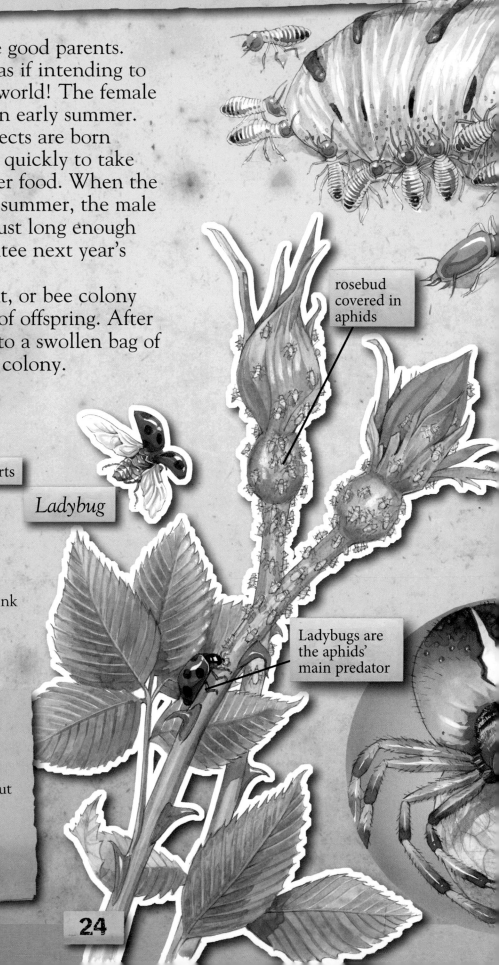

rosebud covered in aphids

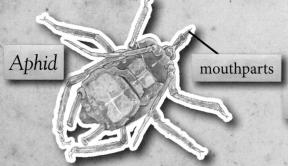

Aphid

mouthparts

Ladybug

Ladybugs are the aphids' main predator

▲ Aphids land on plant stems and drink the sugary liquid meant for the plant's leaves and flowers. Aphids ruin many crops by starving plants in this way.

FACTFILE
APHIDS
- There are 4,000 species of aphids.
- Female aphids produce young without mating. This is called parthenogenesis (virgin birth).
- One aphid can have as many as 25 offspring every day, and billions of descendants in its lifetime!

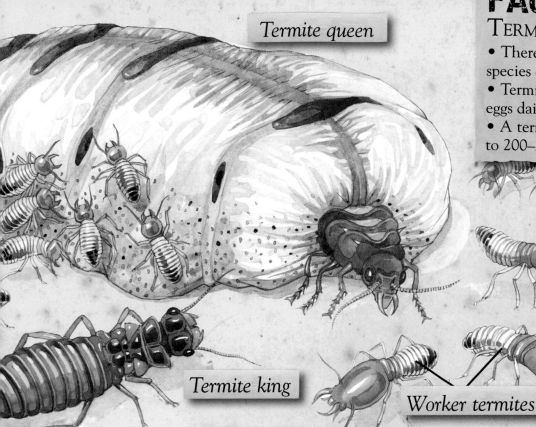

Termite queen

FACTFILE
TERMITES

• There are about 2,000 different species of termite.
• Termite queens can lay 86,400 eggs daily.
• A termite queen's abdomen expands to 200–300 times its pre-pregnant size.

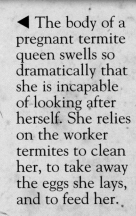

◀ The body of a pregnant termite queen swells so dramatically that she is incapable of looking after herself. She relies on the worker termites to clean her, to take away the eggs she lays, and to feed her.

Termite king

Worker termites

▼ A wolf spider mother puts her eggs in a sac of silk and attaches it behind her body. The female carries her newly hatched young on her abdomen for a while. Often she will care for her youngsters until she dies.

▲ The mating behavior of spiders differs widely between species. Often, the female eats the male after mating. So, a spider surrounded by babies is almost always female.

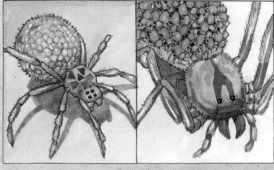

▲ Once the eggs are fertilized, they mature in the female's body. Spider mothers take great care of their offspring. They often carry the eggs or the young on their abdomen to protect them.

▲ Many spider mothers put their eggs in a sac of silk and guard them until they hatch. A few species of spider produce offspring who eat their mother shortly after hatching.

▲ The eggs of *Araneus diadematus* are laid in a ball, in plant stems. When they are ready to hatch, the slightest touch causes the ball to explode, releasing the tiny spiders.

Wolf spider

silk egg sac

Unwanted Passengers

Some bugs are parasites and pests. They live on other animals, sucking their blood and using them for warmth and shelter. This is fine for the bug, but not so lucky for its victim. The bites of mosquitoes, fleas, and ticks can be very painful and can get infected. Mosquito bites can pass on deadly diseases such as malaria. Bugs that bite us live with us, in our clothes, in our beds, and in our hair—and being clean is no guarantee of escaping their attentions.

Dog Flea

FACTFILE
PARASITES AND PESTS
- The largest flea, *Hystrichopsylla schefferi*, is almost half an inch (11 mm) long.
- Lice have been on Earth for 130 million years.
- The eggs of a human head louse are known as "nits."
- In South America, the bite of the assassin bug spreads a deadly disease.

▶ Dog and cat fleas do not live on people, but they can bite us. Only human lice can pass disease between people. The worst case was in Russia between 1918 and 1922, when 3 million people died after catching a disease spread by lice.

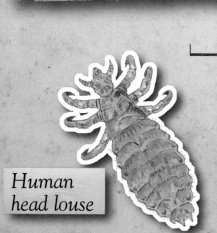

Human head louse

Book louse

Bedbug

▲ Human head lice have no wings and cannot fly. They jump from head to head and cling to their hosts using their well-developed claws.

▲ *Liposcelis divinatorius*, the book louse, feeds on the mold that grows in old, damp books. It damages the paper in the process.

▲ Bedbugs feed on human blood and live in mattresses and bedding. They expand to 3 or 4 times their normal size as their gut fills with blood.

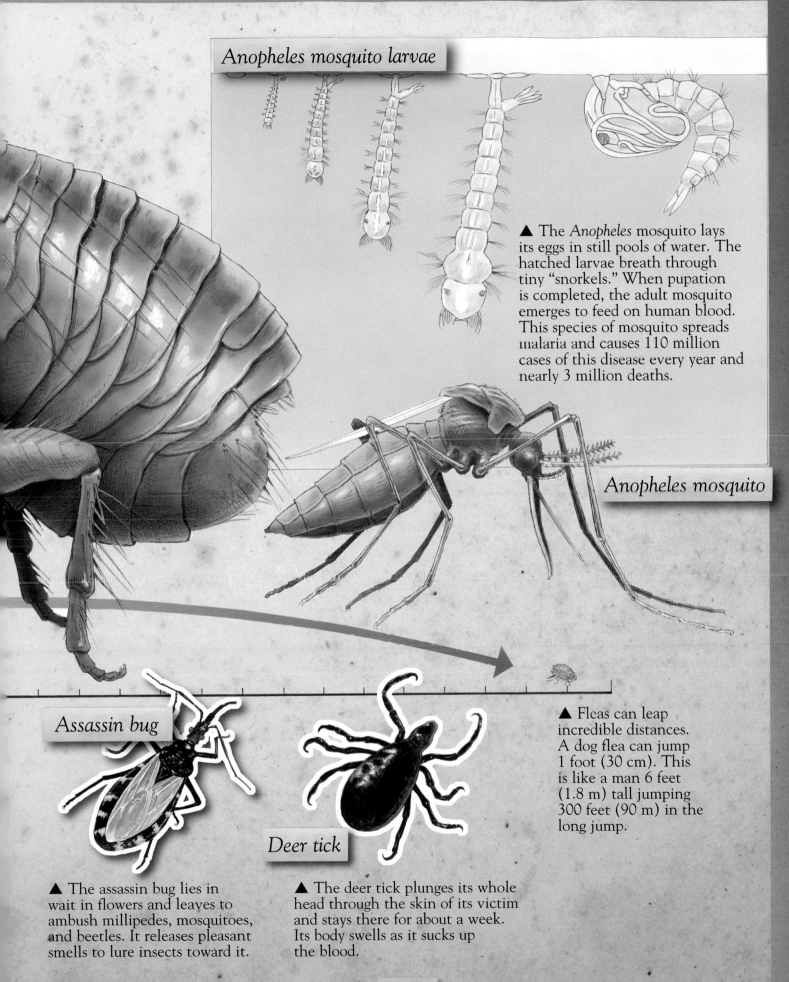

Anopheles mosquito larvae

▲ The *Anopheles* mosquito lays its eggs in still pools of water. The hatched larvae breath through tiny "snorkels." When pupation is completed, the adult mosquito emerges to feed on human blood. This species of mosquito spreads malaria and causes 110 million cases of this disease every year and nearly 3 million deaths.

Anopheles mosquito

Assassin bug

Deer tick

▲ Fleas can leap incredible distances. A dog flea can jump 1 foot (30 cm). This is like a man 6 feet (1.8 m) tall jumping 300 feet (90 m) in the long jump.

▲ The assassin bug lies in wait in flowers and leaves to ambush millipedes, mosquitoes, and beetles. It releases pleasant smells to lure insects toward it.

▲ The deer tick plunges its whole head through the skin of its victim and stays there for about a week. Its body swells as it sucks up the blood.

Invisible Bugs

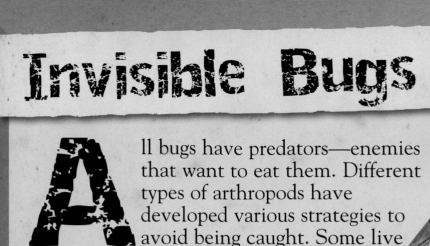

All bugs have predators—enemies that want to eat them. Different types of arthropods have developed various strategies to avoid being caught. Some live in colonies in elaborate nests. Others have strong defenses—perhaps fierce mouthparts and venom. Still others contain bad-tasting chemicals or poison that make them impossible to eat. The bugs on these two pages blend into the background so well that their predators miss them. You might have trouble spotting them, too. Take a look—every bug mentioned is hidden on these pages.

Geomantis larvoides

▲ The mantis *Geomantis larvoides* has evolved to look like a piece of old wood. It is not as glamorous as many of the other mantises, but it is easily mistaken for a seed pod, or a dead twig or leaf.

Praying mantis

▶ The common European praying mantis has a stick-like green body that helps it to camouflage itself from predators. It gets its name because its two front limbs are always slightly bent and it looks as though it is kneeling to pray.

Crestal mantis

▶ This mantis mimics the appearance of broad green leaves. Its attack is quick and deadly. The neck of the prey is chewed to paralyze it, and then the mantis eats the rest of the body.

Lappet moth

▶ Lappet moths look like fall leaves. The larvae feed on poplar, aspen, and willow trees. They overwinter as pupae and hatch into moths in the spring.

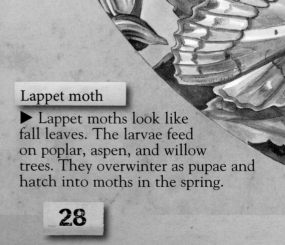

Stick insect

◄ The giant stick insect, usually known as the walking-stick, eats the leaves of oaks and other hardwoods. It escapes predators by looking exactly like the twigs that it sits on. Adults can grow to 3 inches (75mm) long

Leaf insect

◄ Some stick insects, rather than imitating twigs and sticks, have evolved to look like the leaves in which they hide. The edges of a leaf insect's body even look as though an animal has chewed them.

Orchid mantis

◄ The orchid mantis has one of the most fantastic disguises of all. Its body is elaborately folded and the swollen and strongly colored limbs make it appear exactly like local exotic orchids.

Bug Quiz

1. To which section of an insect are the legs attached?
   a) The head
   b) The thorax
   c) The abdomen

2. What percentage of all the animals in the world are beetles?
   a) 25%
   b) 50%
   c) 5%

3. What is the wingspan of an adult female Queen Alexandra birdwing?
   a) About 5 inches (13 cm)
   b) About 12 inches (30 cm)
   c) About 24 inches (60 cm)

4. How long do some American cicada larvae live underground?
   a) 17 weeks
   b) 17 months
   c) 17 years

5. What is the maximum number of legs a millipede can have?
   a) 750
   b) 1000
   c) 100

6. What are the most destructive insects in the world?
   a) Locusts
   b) Furniture beetles
   c) Book lice

7. What do silkworms eat?
   a) Gooseberry leaves
   b) Blackberry leaves
   c) Mulberry leaves

8. What type of insect is born pregnant?
   a) The termite queen
   b) The female aphid
   c) The queen bee

9. How many eggs does a termite queen lay every day?
   a) 46,800
   b) 64,800
   c) 86,400

10. What part of a plant do walking-stick insects look like?
    a) A twig
    b) A leaf
    c) A flower

Quiz answers

1) b   see page 7
2) a   see page 10
3) b   see page 13
4) c   see page 15
5) a   see page 17
6) a   see page 19
7) c   see page 23
8) b   see page 24
9) c   see page 25
10) a   see page 29

Glossary

abdomen The part of the body of an arthropod that usually contains the digestive system and reproductive organs.

arachnids A subgroup of the arthropods that includes spiders.

arthropods The class of animals that includes insects, spiders, centipedes, and millipedes. Arthropods do not have a backbone and they have a tough exoskeleton. Their bodies are divided into sections. Insects have three: head, thorax, and abdomen.

book lungs The breathing organs of an arachnid.

carnivore An animal that kills other animals for food.

cephalothorax The head and thorax of a spider, which are fused together.

cocoon The silk casing in which a butterfly or moth pupates.

complete metamorphosis A life cycle in which the larva pupates when it has grown big enough. The larva and the adult stages of the life cycle usually look completely different.

compound eye An eye made up of many units. Compound eyes usually have many lenses, unlike a human eye which only contains one.

cuticle The outer layer of an arthropod exoskeleton that protects the body from drying out.

dorsal On the back of an animal. The red and black markings on a ladybug, for example, can be seen on its dorsal surface.

exoskeleton The outer, hard armor that supports and protects the body of an arthropod.

herbivore An animal that eats mostly plants.

incomplete metamorphosis A life cycle in which an egg hatches into a nymph. It does not pupate.

invertebrate An animal without a backbone. All insects, spiders, centipedes, and millipedes are invertebrates.

larva (plural: **larvae**) A young form of an animal that does not look like the adult. Some arthropods hatch from eggs into larvae before becoming a pupa. A caterpillar, for example, is the larva of a butterfly.

nocturnal More active in the night than in the day. Most moths are nocturnal.

nymph A young form of an animal that hatches from an egg and looks like a small version of the adult.

parasite An animal that lives on another animal, and harms it.

parthenogenesis Reproduction without fertilization.

phylum One of the major subdivisions that scientists use to classify the animal kingdom.

predator An animal that hunts another animal for food.

prey An animal that is hunted by another animal for food.

pupa A larva bound into a pupa, or cocoon, during complete metamorphosis. After **pupating** for a few days, the adult emerges.

regurgitated food Partly digested food given by some animals to their young.

sterile Unable to produce offspring.

thorax The middle body section of an insect. The legs and wings are usually attached to it.

venom A poison produced by an animal.

ventral On the underside of an animal's body.

Index